LIVING WITH
CANCER AND *Jesus*
Hope and Encouragement for
Those Living with Cancer

By

Kathy R. Graff

Scriptures taken from the Holy Bible, New International Version®, NIV®.
Copyright © 1973, 1978, 1984, 2011 by Biblica, Inc.™ Used by permission of
Zondervan. All rights reserved worldwide. www.zondervan.com The "NIV"
and "New International Version" are trademarks registered in the United States
Patent and Trademark Office by Biblica, Inc.™ All rights reserved.

2nd Edition
Cover photo by author
ISBN: 978-1-7267-3372-4

Acknowledgements

I would like to share a heartfelt thank you to the
following people for their love, prayers and
encouragement during my time with cancer
and help with the production
and marketing of this book.

My Family
Mary Wolfe
Scott Beattie
Marian Heyman
Taylor Amanda Graff
Elizabeth Nguyen
Elaine Golden
Phillip Buss
Pastor Jose Lopes
Will and Michelle Housley
First Baptist Church, Manchester, CT
Smilow Cancer Hospital, Yale New Haven

This book is dedicated to all those who struggle with cancer

"Now to him who is able to do immeasurably
more than all we ask or imagine,
according to his power that is at work within us,
to him be glory in the church and in
Christ Jesus throughout all generations,
forever and ever! Amen."

Ephesians 3:20-21

We are not victims of cancer
We are children of the Living God

Contents

Introduction

There was a time in my life when I didn't know anyone with cancer. I heard of famous people having it, even distant relatives who had cancer, but for most of my life I had been sheltered from knowing someone who had this disease. It wasn't until 1998 when I had my first "up close and personal" encounter. My mom's sister had bone cancer. We weren't that close, but I remember praying for her before visiting her in the hospital. I had only been a Christian for about four years and to my recollection I had never prayed for someone who had the "Big C" disease we call cancer. In my young Christian life, that required a huge prayer.

I remember where I was when I was saved. It was in the basement of my mom's house. That's where I found Jesus. No, He wasn't hiding under the bed or in the closet. What I mean is I found who He really was. I had been listening to a Baptist preacher on TV for about a year. His name was Charles Stanley. I liked what he was saying. It was the first time I heard that you could have a personal relationship with God through Jesus Christ. I thought to myself, how can that be? With my upbringing in another denomination, I knew in my mind that Jesus died on the cross for my sins and I knew in my mind that He was God's only son, but it was all strictly academic. I have come to realize that there is a difference between head knowledge and heart knowledge. You can fill your head with ideas. You can even fill your head with the knowledge of God. However, unless a truth makes it into your heart, there is no new life. For it is from our hearts that we walk, speak and live God's life of truth.

I had never really read the Bible until a King James Version of the Bible appeared, seemingly out of nowhere, on the coffee table in the living room at my parent's house. I started to read it out of sheer boredom. I didn't like that version. I had a hard time understanding the "thee's" and thou's" and I could never figure out who was talking to whom, but I was still intrigued by it nonetheless. Just as abruptly as it had appeared, the Bible eventually disappeared. Despite my difficulties in reading it, I was disappointed. I came to the conclusion that it must have belonged to a friend of my moms who was staying with us temporarily.

My sister, who was a Christian and a member of the Salvation Army Church, gave me a New International Version (NIV) of the Bible. This was a much more user-friendly version. And there began my search in the scriptures for Jesus. In the beginning, I wasn't a fan of the Old Testament (OT) because I thought God was cruel and harsh. He seemed like a "kinder, gentler" God in the New Testament (NT) because of Jesus. So, for a while, I would read only the NT, in particular the gospels which had Christ's words in red. When I came to the end of the Gospel of John, I was very disappointed. Not because of what I had previously read, but because the red letters were gone. At first, I wondered where Jesus went. I wanted to read more straight from the mouth of Jesus. Not from some letter some guy wrote to some church. I remember one time as I lay in bed late at night reading the book of Matthew, a particular scripture stood out among the rest.

"Come to me, all you who are weary and burdened, and I will give you rest. Take my yoke upon you and learn from me, for I am gentle and humble in heart, and you will find rest for your souls. For my yoke is easy and my burden is light." Matthew 11:28-30

The scripture seemed to jump off the page. I felt like Jesus was talking directly to me.

After reading the Bible on my own for several months, I came to love it. I couldn't put it down. I read straight through the NT. I eventually went back and read the OT, and in time I fell in love with the God of the Bible. I began to realize that the OT consisted of prophecies about Christ, and the NT was the fulfillment of those prophecies.

During this time of discovering Jesus, I was going through some difficult times in my life. One night I went into my room, closed the door and knelt at my bed and sobbed. I told God that I didn't know how to pray to Him, so I was just going to talk. I told Him how frustrated and tired of life I was. I listed things about myself that I knew he wasn't happy with, and quite frankly, I was pretty sick and tired of myself. But I couldn't change them. I told Him that I not only needed His help, but I needed Him. At that point, I knew in my heart that Jesus Christ was the only way to the God of the Universe. I didn't ask Christ into my life. I just told Him to take it and do something with it because it was going nowhere fast. After sobbing, I promptly got up, dried my eyes and went to bed with a peace I had never known before. In retrospect, I believe that this was the first promise in the Bible I experienced.

"And when you pray, do not be like the hypocrites, for they love to pray standing in the synagogues and on the street corners to be seen by men. I tell you the truth; they have received their reward in full. But when you pray, go into your room, close the door and pray to your Father, who is unseen. Then your Father, who sees what is done in secret, will reward you. And when you pray, do not keep on babbling like pagans, for they think they will be heard because of their many words. Do not be like them, for your Father knows what you need before you ask him." Matthew 6:5-8.

That is when I found that it was ok to pour out my heart to God, for He hears and knows all things, even before we know it. After some time, I started praying for little things. Not big things. I thought maybe I should start small and see where it goes. Well, after seeing just about every prayer being answered, I figured maybe I need to talk to someone who is likeminded. It was about one year after I was saved that I started seeking a Bible Study to be involved with. I found one at a church on Sunday morning near our house. I was determined that I was only going for the Bible study. God had different plans. I joined a women's study and it was great. We all shared what we had discovered in God's word and what it meant. Then someone asked if we had any prayer requests. I was not up on any of the language, so I asked what a prayer request was. They said if I had a need, they would pray that God would meet that need. I told them I needed a job and that I had been on unemployment for about four months. We all prayed. That was March of 1993. I got a job the next month. Needless to say, I am still with the same church.

When my aunt was diagnosed with cancer, my mom wanted me to give her a book by Max Lucado called "When God Whispers Your Name". As I drove to the hospital, I prayed that God would heal her and I hoped that she knew Christ as her Savior. I didn't want to go and beat her over the head with the Bible, but as I went to visit her, I couldn't help think that it would be great to have some kind of hint that she was going to heaven. When I saw her, she didn't look that bad. She was fairly upbeat. I gave her the book mom wanted her to have. She said out loud the name of the book and told me that with everything going on she hadn't thanked God for her life and her family. She was so humble and peaceful. I said to her, "I think you just told Him." We talked a little more about our memories together. Then I said goodbye and left with such a peace in my heart that she was ready to go. Shortly after that, she passed on, but inside my heart I was rejoicing for her. I believed that she was finally healed on the other side of heaven in the arms of Christ. I believe that God answered my prayer.

All of this is to say how my life has changed since Christ came into it. I became a believer in prayer, scripture, Jesus Christ and His church. I know with confidence that Jesus has given me new life, a place in His eternal kingdom and a purpose in this life. Little did I know that all this time He was preparing me for something far bigger than anything I could handle on my own, something I never in a million years thought would happen to me. This brings me to the point of this book.

In August of 2011 I was diagnosed with muscle invasive bladder cancer. I felt encouraged by the Lord and friends at church to begin a blog about my journey with cancer and Christ. It is an online diary of the daily fear that comes with cancer along with the grace and power of God that helped me through it. I felt compelled by the Lord to turn the blog into a book.

In reading this book, my prayer for you is to find peace in your daily struggles, whatever they may be in your life. Perhaps, like my story, you are suffering from a cancer or other disease that is ravaging your body. Maybe it is the emotional stress of having lost a job or a loved one. It may even be the torture of a guilt-ridden life that may cause you to believe God could never forgive you. I pray that you find freedom from fear, hope from helplessness and joy in Jesus in your situation. This book is not so much about me or my cancer as it is about my Father in heaven who is in complete control of all that happens to us in this life, about my Savior Jesus Christ who bore my sin and is preparing a place for me in his kingdom, and the Holy Spirit who dwells in my heart and is the great comforter.

"In my distress I called to the LORD; I cried to my God for help. From his temple he heard my voice; my cry came before him, into his ears." Psalm 18:6

CHAPTER 1

An Extra Centimeter of Grace

My journey with cancer began in 2008 when I was diagnosed with a stage three tumor in my right kidney. It started with a routine blood test that indicated an abnormal kidney function. I went through a string of medical tests only to find a five centimeter in diameter object in my right kidney which was already abnormally small. It seems my kidney had shriveled down to about six centimeters, one half the size of a normal kidney. After meeting with several doctors, it was determined that I had been living on one kidney for several years, possibly due to a birth defect. We don't know for sure.

Between tests and waiting periods, it was several weeks before we had an answer as to what the object was. If you have ever experienced waiting for test results from the doctor's office, especially waiting to hear if you have cancer, you know exactly what I mean. "What if" thoughts go running through your mind. You start thinking about death and how you are

> God does not always give us the answer we want to hear, when we want to hear it. But he is always there ready to give the peace and grace needed to go through it.

going to tell your family. I actually made a list of songs I would want the praise band to play at my funeral. I was determined that I wanted it to be a time of celebration, not a time of sadness. After all, I knew where I was going. I reasoned in my mind that if I started planning, I wouldn't be shocked by the report.

Although I felt secure in where I was going should the tests prove the worst case scenario, the thought of dying is still fearful. Death is the final battle where Satan tries to do the most damage. He tries to break your spirit and cast doubts in your mind. And if you entertain those "what if" thoughts too long you are going down. The greatest damage control known to man is on his knees with the Bible in his hands.

I remember it as if it were yesterday. It was my 49th birthday. My mind was consumed with "what if" notions. I felt like I was wavering back and forth between faith and fear. I had in my mind that if this was truly bad news, this would be a great opportunity to show others the grace of God in my life, only to have fear overtake my mind with the thought that I did something to displease my Lord. I thought He didn't love me anymore and was going to strike me dead with cancer. Fortunately, that thought did not last long. I knew the word of God. I knew very well that He loved me and that I was sealed in His love through my faith in Christ.

"And you also were included in Christ when you heard the word of truth, the gospel of your salvation. Having believed, you were marked in him with a seal, the promised Holy Spirit, who is a deposit guaranteeing our inheritance until the redemption of those who are God's possession to the praise of his glory." Ephesians 1:13-14.

It was a night of emotional ups and downs. I finally got on my knees and wept before the Lord. I told Him that waiting for this test result wasn't working out for me and how frightened I was. Then, I confessed my lack of trust in Him. It was at this point when my way of thinking turned around. It is amazing what confession and true repentance does for you almost immediately. Your mind clears and you feel like you have a fresh start. God in His grace through the cross of Jesus Christ offers unlimited forgiveness. That doesn't give us the freedom to sin, but the freedom not to sin. The blood that was shed by Jesus on the cross is the only power that can break us free from the deadly cycle of our own sinful habits.

Eventually, I found myself surrendering my circumstance to the living God of the Universe. I prayed the promise He made to us all. I asked for the "peace of God which transcends all understanding, will guard your hearts and your minds in Christ Jesus" (Philippians 4:7). I knew there was only one place to go, on my knees. I knew there was only one person that could give me the peace I needed. That was Jesus Christ.

By the time 1:00am rolled around, I was still tossing and turning. The thought entered my mind to log onto the Worship Network on the internet. Years ago, I would fall asleep watching it on television. Sometimes the Lord would wake me in the middle of the night to tell me something through the devotionals and the scriptures. It had been several years since our cable company stopped airing the network. The many attempts to get the 24 hour live feed on my old, failing computer was futile. So, I dismissed the idea of trying. For 20 minutes I tried to shake the suggestion, but to no avail it would not leave my mind. So, I caved in and gave it a shot. I logged onto the Network, clicked on the live feed, and to my amazement it came right on with no hesitation, no crashing. Once again, I changed my way of thinking.

This reminds me of the story of the miraculous catch of fish in John 21. The disciples went fishing at night and caught nothing.

"Early in the morning, Jesus stood on the shore, but the disciples did not realize that it was Jesus. He called out to them, 'Friends haven't you any fish?' 'No,' they answered. He said, 'Throw your net on the right side of the boat and you will find some.' When they did, they were unable to haul the net in because of the large number of fish." John 21:4-6

I wonder what the disciples thought when Jesus told them to throw the net on the other side of the boat. They were fishermen. They knew what they were doing. Of course they said no, (and of course, I was determined that the live feed on the computer was not going to work). Much to their amazement, their nets were full of fish. And when they saw it was Jesus, their hearts were filled with praise and adoration. Oh how important it is that we act on what the Lord tells us to do. I cannot begin to count the number of blessings I missed because I did not act on the Lord's word.

At 1:30am sharp one of the worship leaders came on and shared a devotional about a woman named Kathy who gave up a kidney. Of course my reaction was nothing short of shock and awe, both at the same time. Although her circumstance was quite different than mine, I got the message. I have had the Lord speak to me several times through Bible studies, sermons and other Christians in the past, but not through something that literally had my name on it, let alone the same organ in question. My initial reaction was the same as it always is, "You have got to be kidding me! Oh, come on! Give me a break!" Rest assured that these statements are never made from disbelief, but from amazement. At this point I was trying to decide in my own mind if God was telling me that He was going to take my kidney.

Afterwards, scriptures started scrolling on the screen to which I started weeping before God, this time out of gratitude, humbleness and peace, instead of fear and feeling forsaken. Many of the scriptures had to do with His peace. Among them, two stand out to this day.

"Peace I leave with you; my peace I give you. I do not give to you as the world gives. Do not let your hearts be troubled and do not be afraid." John 14:27

"I have told you these things, so that in me you may have peace. In this world you will have trouble. But take heart! I have overcome the world." John 16:33

There is nothing like the supernatural peace of God that overcomes your entire being. In context, Jesus is comforting and encouraging his disciples as he is about to approach his own death. Jesus knew exactly what each and every one of them would encounter in their lives. He also knows what each of us will encounter. Even though we did not know for sure if it was cancer yet, at this point it didn't matter. I was now convinced that God was going to take my kidney and I was going to be alright.

How often it is that our Lord wants to tell us something, but we just don't take the time to listen. Sometimes it's not so much us calling on Him and waiting for an answer as it is the Lord having the answer and waiting for us to quiet down long enough to hear. We are either so busy with our lives, or we allow sin to creep in and take the place of the sweet, intimate fellowship our Father in heaven desires to have with us. We think giving Him 15 minutes a day is an accomplishment, when really He owns the whole 24/7. Even at 1:30 in the morning.

I remember the day my doctor called me at work to tell me it was cancer. As he told me over the phone, I could feel my heart starting to pound and my blood pressure spike. But it wasn't long until he explained to me what I already knew. Although they had to remove the kidney, the prognosis was good because the cancer was encapsulated. My response was tears of rejoice. That's right. I rejoiced. The tears were not because I was losing my kidney, but because this just confirmed to me that everything was going according to what God had impressed on my heart late that night on my 49th birthday.

God does not always give us the answer we want to hear, when we want to hear it. But He is always there ready to give the peace and grace needed to go through it. Our Lord wants us to have the confidence to come to him. He wants us to be honest before him and to cry out to Him from the depths of our pain and fear. In this, we can experience the hope, peace and comfort that can only come from the throne of grace.

"Therefore, since we have a great high priest who has gone through the heavens, Jesus the Son of God, let us hold firmly to the faith we profess. For we do not have a high priest who is unable to sympathize with our weaknesses, but we have one who has been tempted in every way, just as we are -yet was without sin. Let us then approach the throne of grace with confidence, so that we may receive mercy and find grace to help us in our time of need." Hebrews 4:4-16

Jesus is our High Priest. We can have confidence to come before Him with our petitions. Why? Because He is the one who died for us. He understood what it was like to be tempted, but was able to walk away without succumbing to those temptations. So, He is there to help us in our time of need whether it is during a time of temptation or a time of fear. Remember, it was after I confessed to God that I did not trust Him with my situation that things turned around. It was after my repentance that He answered me with mercy and grace in my time of need.

Prayer Letter

Dear God;

You know what I am going through. I confess I cannot handle this myself. Forgive me for not trusting you. I submit my circumstance to you right now.

With all my thanksgiving,

_____

Your name

"Consider what God has done: Who can straighten what he has made crooked? When times are good, be happy; but when times are bad, consider: God has made the one, as well as the other. Therefore, a man cannot discover anything about his future."
Ecclesiastes 7:14

CHAPTER 2

Another Visit

Life is good. I have my family which consists of three sisters and a brother, all of whom are married and I try to visit my mom every year in South Carolina. And, let's not forget the 13 nieces and nephews (as of this writing) which are the brightest sparkle in my eye. I absolutely love hearing "Auntie Rose" from each and every one of them (Rose is my middle name). I don't think God could have put me with a better family. I have my friends at work who are always a great support. Then there is my church family. I couldn't ask for better brothers and sisters in the body of Christ to be linked with. They are true prayer warriors. They are far greater prayer warriors than I.

Yes, life was good. It was now the year 2011. I was down one kidney, but I was cancer free- or so I thought. Little did I know that another cancer was hiding incognito. The dictionary defines incognito as "having one's identity concealed, as under an assumed name, especially to avoid notice or formal attentions." Well, it hid from me and the doctors for some time. I began to notice symptoms of a Urinary Tract Infection (UTI) in April. I was tested several times which was followed with antibiotics. Sometimes the test came back

> As it is written in the book of Ecclesiastes, God is the author of the good times and the bad times involving our lives. If he is the author of both, then he is the finisher of both.

positive for UTI, sometimes it did not. The problem was that the symptoms of UTI persisted and even got worse. Antibiotics were not making a difference. There was increased blood in my urine.

By the time I could get to my urologist to get checked out, it was August. Much to his shock and amazement, he said I had a tumor in my bladder. Of course panic ensued. The following week I found myself in surgery to have the tumor removed. The problem was that it was too big to take the whole thing out. So, he only took out part of it to send out for a biopsy. There's that word again. The big "B" word which stands for biopsy, that usually is followed by the big "C" word, cancer.

Again, I had to wait almost two weeks for the report. I was determined that I was going to handle this well. Why not! I'd been through this before. I can do it again. Well, that wasn't the case. It was finally "D-day", or "B-day" (for biopsy). While I was waiting for the doctor to come in with the report, I felt my nerves starting to kick in. I prayed and asked God to give me the grace and peace to handle whatever the outcome was.

It seemed like I was waiting forever before the doctor finally came in. He asked me how I was doing and I told him I was fine. Then he dropped the "C-bomb". He said the bad news is I have a very rare and aggressive bladder cancer called squamous cell carcinoma. It looks to be at least a stage two, but won't know for sure until the bladder is removed. I asked about chemo and radiation and he said this type of cell does not react to either. Then he dropped the big "W" word, which stands for my weight. The news seemed to be going from bad to worse. He said it will be very difficult to remove the bladder with my weight and that the survival rate was low. We agreed that I would see the oncologist. We set up an appointment and that was that. It was quick and decisive. This is what it is and this is how bad it is. I could die.

Before I could call my family, I had to sit in the parking lot for a while to process what I just heard. My heart was pounding so hard, it felt like it was trying to push its way outside of my chest. This was the same doctor who took out my kidney in 2008 via laparoscopic surgery. He had a far better outlook back then. This was very different. To remove my bladder would mean a full open surgery.

No one knew what was growing inside of me except God. By God's perfect and sovereign will, I had bladder cancer. If that sounds strange to you, you are not alone. But if there is one thing I have learned in this journey, it is that God is always working on my behalf, regardless of the circumstance.

As it is written in the book of Ecclesiastes, God is the author of the good times and the bad times involving our lives. If He is the author of both, then He is the finisher of both. And none of us can know His purpose until we go through the circumstance and come out on the other side. Until then, we must trust him. And that requires an extra measure of grace from God, and an extra measure of faith on my part.

Prayer Letter

Dear God;

You know everything that is going on in my life and everything that is to come. Nothing shocks you. Please help me to stand firm in you. Hold me up when I feel faint in the midst of my fear and desperation.

Trusting in you,

_____

Your name

"Now I know that the LORD saves his anointed; he answers him from his Holy heaven with the saving power of his right hand. Some trust in chariots and some in horses, but we trust in the name of the LORD our God. They are brought to their knees and fall, but we rise up and stand firm." Psalm 20:6-8

CHAPTER 3

Trust in Chariots and Horses?

I began my quest to find someone who could save my bladder. My sister Wendy came with me on my visit to the first oncologist. She was a trooper. She had pen and paper in hand, determined to get all the facts. I knew I couldn't get them. After all, it was my life on the line. It was my future we would be discussing. I couldn't think straight. To this day I barely remember what was said in that room.

The oncologist came in with a pen and file in hand. That much I remember. It seemed he wasn't offering much information aside from answering questions presented to him. He said it would be difficult to do the surgery because of my weight, as if the news that it was cancer wasn't bad enough. Wendy wrote down the stages of bladder cancer as he read them off. For each increased stage, the percentage rate of the cancer reoccurring grew. Then he confirmed what the surgeon had said previously. Squamous cell does not react to traditional chemo or radiation. My hope was slowly being chipped away.

> The cross is the only bridge to God's throne room. Jesus' death reconciles us to God and allows us to enter into a personal, intimate relationship with our heavenly Father. Religion won't cut it when you are stuck in a black hole of despair.

We told him we had a list of other hospitals that we wanted to get a second and third opinion from. He thought it would be a good idea, but not to wait too long. He said the tumor was big and that we shouldn't wait more than about 4-6 weeks. I am glad Wendy was there. If there was one thing about her, she was strong. Her attitude was "let's get the facts and then attack this thing."

Before I continue on this track, I just want to say that having your family there to support you is a major part of getting through cancer. My whole family has been awesome. In your journey with your cancer I hope you have that kind of family support. God puts people in our lives to encourage us. Do not be afraid to ask for help. My church family has been a great support as well. Between the church and my own family, I had a lot of people praying for me. That's important too.

I decided to go to the next hospital by myself. I figured I knew enough already so nothing would shock me. I figured wrong. The next doctor told me the same thing but with one more piece of information I could have done without. He said that squamous cell is almost always fatal. Not what I wanted to hear. So I left that office not feeling much better. Suddenly I found myself leaving the path of trying to save my bladder to desperately running the path of finding someone who would actually do the surgery, with confidence despite the overwhelming risks from my weight.

I finally went to a third hospital outside of my state. This doctor said the same thing. Again, I have an almost fatal disease.

I must admit, at that point I was getting angry. I was emotionally and physically exhausted. My sister-in-law, Heidi drove me to the appointment. That was a great blessing. Then three of my close friends from church came out for support. I really needed it then. I could feel a deep sense of discouragement settling in. I had one more hospital on my list and I was running out of steam fast. My deacon at church suggested Smilow Cancer Hospital at Yale. I didn't even know Yale had a cancer facility. I told him it wasn't on my list, but that I would think about it.

As I went through the motions of looking for other opinions, I found my focus was in the wrong place. Through another person's testimony, I knew the Lord was asking me a crucial question. My answer would determine which direction my faith would go. Was I going to put my trust in the three doctors who offered no hope, or would I trust in Him, my only hope? Sometimes it's easier to answer that question than to live it out. Of course I chose to trust God.

Now I am not against doctors. Neither is God. We all have gifts and talents ordained from eternity past. God knew our vocations before we were born. Look at the apostle Luke. He was a physician. If he didn't know his limitations, I am sure he saw them once he learned of Jesus' healing power. God uses doctors to heal with the knowledge He gives them, whether they are aware of it or not.

Up to this point I had not received a word from God that was as clear as the message I received with my kidney cancer. That was incredible. This time around, I hadn't heard anything to the tune of "Kathy, you are going to lose your bladder, but you are going to be ok." God was silent on that front.

Along with the uncertainty of my future, there were great times of deep fear. It didn't matter where I was. I would be at work, with my family, at church or at home and it would come on me all of a sudden without any warning. I would find myself being overcome with a paralyzing fear that words just can't explain and I would start crying uncontrollably. If it were possible for a human being to be sucked into a black hole and still be conscious that might describe it.

Fortunately, if that were true, there is nowhere in the universe any of us could escape the presence of God. In those darkest moments of fear, I found myself praying to God in a way I never had before. I asked the Lord, by His Holy Spirit, to remove this spirit of fear so I could function again. In seconds I felt His peace come over my entire being. I would stop crying, dry my eyes and move on from that dark moment.

These are the moments that draw a fine line between faith and religion. God is not seeking people who are religious. They look for ways to please Him in their works. They think they have to be good enough in and of themselves to be accepted by God. Faith in God is trusting that He already accepts us no matter where we are in life in light of the atoning sacrifice Jesus made on our behalf at the cross. It's not about what we do to earn God's love. It is about the love God has shown for us in Christ before the foundation of the world.

"For it is by grace you have been saved, through faith -and this not from yourselves, it is the gift of God - not by works, so that no one can boast." Ephesians 2:8-9

God seeks people who trust Him and that only comes through knowing who God is through Christ. The cross is the only bridge to God's throne room. Jesus' death reconciles us to God and allows us to enter into a personal, intimate relationship with our heavenly Father. Religion won't cut it when you are stuck in a black hole of despair.

To this day, I still tell people that Jesus is the only reason why I didn't check myself into a strait jacket. There is no way I would have been able to get through my cancer without my Heavenly Father's presence.

Eventually, circumstances were arranged by God that left me no choice but to go to Yale. It's funny how that happened. I was working from a list of four high profile hospitals. God was working from His list of one hospital I had never heard of. That was my mistake. I was working from the wrong list.

Prayer Letter

Dear God;

Thank you that there is nowhere I can escape your presence.
Forgive me those times I worked so hard to be accepted by you.
Remind me that I am already accepted at the cross of your Son,
Jesus Christ. Help me to better understand that his sacrifice on
the cross means I can have a personal relationship with you.
Stay near me and help me in my dark moments of despair.

Forever in need of your presence,

_____

Your name

"If any of you lacks wisdom, he should ask God, who gives generously to all without finding fault, and it will be given to him. But when he asks, he must believe and not doubt, because he who doubts is like a wave of the sea, blown and tossed by the wind. That man should not think he will receive anything from the Lord; he is a double-minded man, unstable in all he does." James 1:5-8

CHAPTER 4
Faith or Doubt

Here is a word to the wise. If you ever find yourself in the doctor's office and he tells you that you have a particular disease, do not rush home and get on the internet. That can only make things more challenging for you. There are many so called "medical" websites and a lot of them contradict each other. You will be more confused after you log off your computer than you did before you walked into the doctor's office.

Around the time I was visiting the first three hospitals, I made the mistake of logging onto YouTube to look up bladder cancer. I found a video of a woman from Britain who had the same aggressive bladder cancer as me. She was a Christian as well. The doctors told her that they had to remove her bladder. When they opened her up and saw that the cancer had spread they didn't go any further with the surgery. After, they told her there was nothing they could do for her and that she was going to die. She went to a prayer meeting and needless to say, Jesus stepped in and supernaturally healed her and made her cancer free.

> Just when you have exhausted yourself from running after worldly answers, know that God has been running after you all this time. And when He catches up to you, He will blow you away with His mercy, hold you in His grace, and His love will leave you breathless.

At first, I struggled with how to pray for healing. I was so discouraged after seeing the third doctor, I said to the Lord in my frustration, "Why don't you just heal me supernaturally so I don't have to go through such a dangerous surgery?" Well, that didn't last long. I knew better. First of all, how arrogant of me to assume God would heal me at all? Second, I was in no position to dictate to the God of the Universe how to heal me. Yes, God heals. We read throughout the Bible and see God's compassionate hand as Jesus healed lepers, the blind and deaf, and raised people from the dead. I quickly realized that if I didn't know how God would heal me, then I should pray and ask with a humble heart, not a demanding one. When we pray to the Holy God of the universe, I believe it is the attitude of the heart He looks at first. After searching for an answer, I found the perfect scripture for this prayer.

"A man with leprosy came to him and begged him on his knees, "If you are willing, you can make me clean." Filled with compassion, Jesus reached out his hand and touched the man. "I am willing," he said. "Be clean!" Mark 1:40-41

This man did not doubt Jesus' ability to heal him. Neither did I doubt Jesus' ability to heal me. This man also did not presume anything. "If you are willing" shows that the man was very undemanding and humble. The next five words would prove a great deal about the man's faith. He said, "...you can make me clean." The man is simply stating what he believes as a fact. In other words, "Jesus, if you so desire or, if it pleases you, heal me. I already know you are perfectly capable."

I have heard preachers say, "If you want to be healed, believe God can do it." Then they say that if God doesn't heal you it is because you don't have enough faith. Personally, I don't buy it. Jesus said if you have faith the size of a mustard seed, you can move mountains. The bottom line is God heals those whom he chooses to heal and in the form he chooses to do so. There is another story of Jesus' healing, a little closer to home.

A large crowd followed and pressed around him. And a woman was there who had been subject to bleeding for twelve years. She had suffered a great deal under the care of many doctors and had spent all she had, yet instead of getting better she grew worse. When she heard about Jesus, she came up behind him in the crowd and touched his cloak, because she thought, "if I just touch his clothes, I will be healed." Immediately her bleeding stopped and she felt in her body that she was freed from her suffering.

At once Jesus realized that power had gone out from him. He turned around in the crowd and asked, "Who touched my clothes?"

'You see the people crowding against you," his disciples answered, "and yet you can ask, 'Who touched me?'"

But Jesus kept looking around to see who had done it. Then the woman, knowing what had happened to her, came and fell at his feet and, trembling with fear, told him the whole truth. He said to her, "Daughter, your faith has healed you. Go in peace and be freed from your suffering." Mark 5:24-34

I wonder what was going through the mind of this poor woman. Maybe God asked her the same crucial question He asked me. Maybe He challenged her to trust Jesus instead of the doctors who offered her no hope. After all, this was her last ditch effort to be physically healed. We know the doctors couldn't do anything for her. She was desperate and tired of being bounced from one to the other. None of them could seem to find anything in their arsenal to combat her disease of 12 years. I know exactly how she felt. There were times when I felt like it was all I could do to hang onto God by a thread. But after reading this story I found that a thread of faith was enough.

I just want to bring out a couple of points from this story. First, Jesus was on his way, at the request of a father, to heal his dying daughter. Don't ever think that God is too busy to hear your plea, or cares more for someone else because He got to them first. We are all on the same level before God when it comes to our sin. But we are also on the same level before God when it comes to His love and care. He does not show favoritism in our sin or in his grace. We are all on equal footing.

Secondly, Jesus did not have to know who touched his clothes, nor did the woman have to call out his name for her to be healed. The spiritual connection was already there. Between the woman's faith and Jesus' compassion, the sick and the healer came together. This is how ready our God is to hear our plea and answer our prayers. Make no mistake my dear friend. Jesus knows your name. Your faith is never beyond the reach of his tender heart. He loves you so much.

Both of these people had faith in Jesus' capability to heal. This is quite different from the story of the man whose son was possessed by a demon in the ninth chapter of the Gospel of Mark.

"So they brought him. When the spirit saw Jesus, it immediately threw the boy into a convulsion. He fell to the ground and rolled around, foaming at the mouth. Jesus asked the boy's father, 'How long has he been like this?' 'From childhood,' he answered. 'It has often thrown him into fire or water to kill him. But if you can do anything, take pity on us and help us.' 'If you can'?' said Jesus. 'Everything is possible for him who believes.' Immediately the boy's father exclaimed, 'I do believe; help me overcome my unbelief!'" Mark 9:20-24

If you are struggling with your faith in Jesus, just ask him for it. God is the one who gives us faith. It is a gift from Him to us. He can help you in your unbelief.

Remember, there is nowhere you can go to escape His presence. Just when you have exhausted yourself from running after worldly answers, know that God has been running after you all this time. And when He catches up to you, He will blow you away with His mercy, hold you in His grace, and His love will leave you breathless.

Prayer Letter

Dear God;

Cover me with your grace and mercy. Sometimes I find myself struggling to trust you. There are times when I am so overwhelmed by my circumstance that your presence seems faint to me. Please help me to keep focused on you. Overwhelm me with your grace, mercy and love that I may overcome my moments of unbelief.

Forever in your capable hands,

_____

Your name

"Humble yourselves, therefore, under God's mighty hand, that he may lift you up in due time. Cast all your anxiety on him because he cares for you." 1Peter 5:6-7

CHAPTER 5

Been There, Done That

Cancer can make you struggle with God. I found myself thinking about our Savior in the Garden of Gethsemane. There were times I cried out the same thing Jesus did, "is there any other way".

"Jesus went out as usual to the Mount of Olives and his disciples followed him. On reaching the place, he said to them, "Pray that you will not fall into temptation." He withdrew about a stone's throw beyond them, knelt down and prayed, "Father, if you are willing, take this cup from me; yet not my will, but yours be done." An angel from heaven appeared to him and strengthened him. And being in anguish, he prayed more earnestly, and his sweat was like drops of blood falling to the ground." Luke 22:38-44

The place was the Garden of Gethsemane. The time was late at night, just before Jesus was arrested. This is where Jesus wrestled between his humanity and deity. He was about to take the long walk to the cross where he would die for our sins. He knew he had to go through with the Father's plan of redeeming the world. But still, he was human. The scripture says, "His sweat was like drops of blood".

It is humanly impossible to comprehend the physical, emotional and spiritual torture Jesus was about to endure for the human race. However, we have a Savior who is able to comprehend our own physical, emotional and spiritual pain. I am of the belief that we all have our own spot in the Garden of Gethsemane. This too is the place that we struggle with God. We've been told the plan by the doctors. We've even been given the odds of survival and we don't like it. But we must go through it. There is no escaping the diagnosis or treatment. Jesus is the perfect picture of staying the course on the narrow road, which he calls us to follow him on.

> Jesus was completely and utterly alone in his suffering on the cross. But think about this. Jesus went to the cross so that you could never, ever be abandoned by God in your time of despair and need.

"Enter through the narrow gate. For wide is the gate and broad is the road that leads to destruction and many enter through it. But small is the gate and narrow the road that leads to life, and few find it." Matthew 7:13-14

Jesus was starting to wrap up the Sermon on the Mount in chapter 7 of Matthew. His teachings were radical but life changing. They were also very controversial to the religious leaders of that day and are still controversial today. I would encourage you to read chapters 6 and 7 in the book of Matthew on your own. Let the Lord speak to your heart.

When I decided to trust Christ as my Savior, I also trusted Him to be my Lord. They both must go hand in hand. I needed to trust and give my entire life to him. After all, he sacrificed his entire life for me. I should give him no less of myself. When I placed my faith in Christ, the wide and easy road that was my life became the narrow and hard road that Jesus called me to walk. I'm not saying that life was easy before I met Christ. Actually, it was the opposite. I am saying life is harder when you are called to follow Christ while still in a sinful world. Christ gives us freedom not to sin. But it's a challenge in a fallen world. No human being was or ever will be perfect this side of heaven. Only Christ walked the Holy and perfect walk on earth.

The narrow road which leads to eternal life is the life that Christ calls us to follow. This means walking in obedience to God, just as Christ was obedient, even unto the cross. If we keep going on the easy track of life, not heeding God's commands, then that will lead to our ultimate spiritual destruction, which is separation from God for eternity. Unless of course we choose to believe in Christ's atoning sacrifice on our behalf. Taking the wide road or the easy way out would indicate a life without suffering. But that's impossible in a fallen world. We would do well to look unto Jesus as our supreme example.

When I asked God to heal me supernaturally, in retrospect, I realized I was trying to widen the narrow road Jesus had called me to walk along at this time in my life. And in that request, I was showing my lack of trust in him. If He could raise the dead, heal the blind and deaf, he could certainly protect me from the dangers of a complicated surgery.

Cancer can also make you feel like you have been abandoned by God. The gospel of Mark records Jesus confiding in his friends, "My soul is overwhelmed with sorrow to the point of death." Jesus was anticipating the abandonment he would experience at the cross. After several hours on the cross, he felt not only the searing pain from the torturous beatings and the nails driven through his hands and feet, but he also felt the pain of being forsaken by his Father in heaven for the first time in his existence.

"From the sixth hour until the ninth hour darkness came over all the land. About the ninth hour Jesus cried out in a loud voice, "Eloi, Eloi, lama sabachthani?"—which means, "My God, my God, why have you forsaken me?" Matthew 27:45-46

Jesus became our sin on the cross. This time, there was no angel there to strengthen him. There was no friend to stand by and hold his hand to encourage him. Jesus was completely and utterly alone in his suffering on the cross. But think about this. Jesus went to the cross so that you could never, ever be abandoned by God in your time of despair and need. I found it encouraging that God sent an angel to strengthen Jesus when he was in the garden. Jesus had a horrific job to do and his Father in heaven gave him strength to go through with it.

During my reflection on Jesus in the Garden of Gethsemane, I tried a little imagination exercise. I would imagine myself leaning on my rock of despair in my little corner of the garden, crying out all my doubts and fears to God. Then I would feel something on my shoulder. When I turn around, I see a nail pierced hand there. I look up and it is Jesus. He points to another rock and says, "That was my spot, right over there. You know the place you read about every Easter. I know exactly how you feel. Been there, done that. Take my strength and I will walk you through this." So I stop crying and start leaning on the Rock of my Salvation.

If you are leaning on a rock of despair in the garden, take heart. We have a God who is merciful, compassionate, understanding, loving and full of grace. And he can walk you through anything because he's been there, done that.

Prayer Letter

Dear God;

I love you, O Lord, my strength. The Lord is my rock, my fortress and my deliverer; my God is my rock, in whom I take refuge. He is my shield and the horn of my salvation, my stronghold. Psalm 18:1-2

This is a hard road to walk. Forgive me those times when I let go of your nail scarred hand and try to handle this on my own. I can't do this without you.

Forever praising you,

_____

Your name

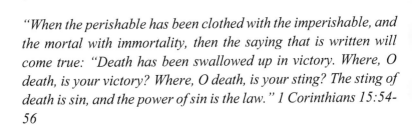

"When the perishable has been clothed with the imperishable, and the mortal with immortality, then the saying that is written will come true: "Death has been swallowed up in victory. Where, O death, is your victory? Where, O death, is your sting? The sting of death is sin, and the power of sin is the law." 1 Corinthians 15:54-56

CHAPTER 6

Death – Where is Your Sting

Here is something I believe God gave me. It goes like this. Cancer represents what is wrong in this fallen, sinful world. Jesus represents all that is right in the universe. One has to be greater than the other.

The National Cancer Institute at the National Institutes of Health gives the following definition of cancer:

"Cancer is a term used for diseases in which abnormal cells divide without control and are able to invade other tissues. Cancer cells can spread to other parts of the body through the blood and lymph systems. The body is made up of many types of cells. These cells grow and divide in a controlled way to produce more cells as they are needed to keep the body healthy. When cells become old or damaged, they die and are replaced with new cells.

> The worst thing that can happen to me is not that I would die, but that I would die without Christ and be separated from God forever. But with Christ as my Lord and savior, that is impossible.

However, sometimes this orderly process goes wrong. The genetic material (DNA) of a cell can become damaged or changed, producing mutations that affect normal cell growth and division. When this happens, cells do not die when they should and new cells form when the body does not need them. The extra cells may form a mass of tissue called a tumor."

We can look at cancer as the disease that it is, a cell spreading out of control in our bodies, or look at it metaphorically as sin that spreads out of control in our spiritual life. God made man perfect starting with Adam and Eve in the Garden of Eden. Within the free will that God gave them, they chose to go off on their own and disobey God and sin entered into the world. Their perfect state ceased to exist. Thus the orderly process of human life went terribly wrong. Humanity took off on a downward spiral from there. Next thing you know, one of their sons, Cain, killed his brother Abel. Not a very good start to the human race.

Just as mutations in our DNA can cause damage in our bodies, our sin can cause damage in our lives as well as other people's lives. Cancer can spread uncontrollably throughout our physical bodies. Let it go unchecked and it could kill us. It's the same thing with our sin. Sin is the spiritual cancer that we are all born with. If left unchecked, it can wreak havoc in every area of our lives. We have no control over either one. Both the cancer and our sin are a result of a fallen world.

The American Cancer Society says that only about five to ten percent of all cancers are hereditary, and that what is inherited is the abnormal gene that causes cancer, not the cancer itself. This is not so about our spiritual state. Every one of us is born with the terminal spiritual disease that is called sin. Doctors continue to strive for a permanent cure for cancer and I am grateful for their efforts. But only one man has the permanent cure for our terminal state of sin, and that's Jesus.

"For the wages of sin is death, but the gift of God is eternal life in Christ Jesus our Lord." Romans 6:23

Jesus himself took on life's final battle, death, when He died on the cross. The deed was done; the punishment that should have been ours was finished. Justice for our sin had been paid in full. And when He victoriously walked out of that tomb on Easter morning, eternal death could no longer claim us.

There is one who holds the universe in His hands and is aware of the cancer that grows in us physically and spiritually. It is by His mercy that we can be healed physically, by his grace that we are forgiven of our sins, and by His love that we are given new life. That is our Savior and Lord Jesus Christ.

"In this world you will have trouble. But take heart! I have overcome the world." John 16:33b.

This is the truth that gave me hope and kept me going during my time with cancer.

A dear friend of mine I had known for 20 years went home to be with the Lord not too long ago. She was a retired school teacher and wonderful woman of God. She was in her late 80's, lived alone, was an incredible bible teacher, loved the Lord and was my personal friend and mentor.

The time came when I and another close friend received the call that she was in the hospital with double pneumonia. For as long as I could remember she always talked about how homesick she was for Heaven. She could not wait to see her Lord. As a matter of fact, when I visited her in the hospital she kept trying to get up out of bed, as frail as she was. When I asked her where she was going, she said home. I asked her, "You're not talking about the nursing home, are you?" She replied as she pointed upwards, "no, a better one." I told her she had to wait on the Lord. She actually wanted to know what was taking so long.

When she was nearing her passing, I and my friend were at her side. Though she strained of trying to breathe from the fluid filling her lungs, she was in no pain, so she required no medication. She was completely aware of her surroundings and was very lucid. Her eyes were closed as we sat by her bedside. We thought she was sleeping. But then she spoke. With her eyes still closed, she said with heavy, deep breathes in between her words, "He is so beautiful." I asked "who, Jesus?" She said yes. I asked "Do you see Him now?" She answered yes. My friend and I just sat there speechless and in awe as we gazed upon her peaceful face. I couldn't help but try to imagine what she was seeing.

After some time of silence in the room she spoke once again, straining for air in between her words. She said, "What we believe is true." That was on a Monday night. She went home to be with the Lord late Tuesday night/Wednesday morning.

This makes me think of what Jesus said to Thomas when he saw Jesus for himself after the resurrection;

"Then Jesus told him, because you have seen me, you have believed; blessed are those who have not seen and yet have believed." John 20:29

In my friend's case, she saw Jesus because she believed. This is the promise He makes to us all who believe by faith. When it comes time to go to our real home in heaven we will look upon the face of the one who gave his life so that we may be free from our sin and spend a blessed eternity with God.

I miss my friend. Sometimes when I walk through my church building I remember seeing her sitting on a bench in her purple winter coat, greeting people as they walked in. I miss our fellowship, but I am so happy for her.

"Brothers and sisters, we do not want you to be uninformed about those who sleep in death, so that you do not grieve like the rest of mankind, who have no hope. For we believe that Jesus died and rose again, and so we believe that God will bring with Jesus those who have fallen asleep in him." 1 Thessalonians 4:13-14

As a Christian I don't see death as a horrible thing. I didn't ask Christ to die on the cross for me. Nobody did. It was God's idea. Why? Because He loved us first. The worst thing that can happen to me is not that I would die, but that I would die without Christ and be separated from God forever. But with Christ as my Lord and Savior, that is impossible.

The story about how Jesus raised Lazarus from the dead is truly amazing. I would encourage you to read the entire story in John 11:1-44. In this account, Martha, one of Lazarus' sisters, believed that her brother would come alive on resurrection day, to which Jesus replied;

"I am the resurrection and the life. He who believes in me will live, even though he dies; and whoever lives and believes in me will never die. Do you believe this?" John 11:25-26

You may be reading this book because you have cancer. You may not know Jesus Christ as the Son of God who sacrificed His life for you. I implore you; trust Jesus and what He did at the cross for you. Confess to God that you are a sinner and need a Savior. Believe that Jesus is the genuine article. Ask God to forgive you in light of what Jesus did at the cross and He will. There is nothing that you have done or ever will do that hasn't been forgiven at the cross.

Prayer Letter

Dear God;

I know there are things in my life that you so desperately want to change or do away with all together. I confess that I want to get rid of some of them as well. I understand it starts with trusting your Son as my Lord and Savior. So here I am Lord, at your feet asking for mercy on my life, forgiveness for all my sins, and a changed life in Christ. Thank you for loving me enough to send Your only Son as the atoning sacrifice for my sin.

Forever praising you,

_____

Your name

"God is our (my) refuge and strength, an ever-present help in trouble". Psalm 46:1

CHAPTER 7

His Promise – Psalm 46

During a rough time the day before my surgery, God reminded me of who He really is.

"God is our (my) refuge and strength, an ever-present help in
trouble. Therefore we (I) will not fear, though the earth give
way and the mountains fall into the heart of the sea,
though its waters roar and foam
and the mountains quake with their surging.

There is a river whose streams make glad the city of God,
the holy place where the Most High dwells.
God is within her, she will not fall;
God will help her at break of day.
Nations are in uproar, kingdoms fall;
He lifts His voice, the earth melts.

The Lord Almighty is with us (me);
the God of Jacob is our (my) fortress.

Come and see the works of the Lord, the desolations He has
brought on the earth. He makes wars cease to the ends of the
earth; He breaks the bow and shatters the spear,
He burns the shields with fire.

'Be still, and know that I am God; I will be exalted among the nations, I will be exalted in the earth.'

The LORD Almighty is with us (me); the God of Jacob is our (my) fortress." Psalm 46

There are times that life hits us so hard that we feel like the whole world is crumbling around us, as described in the beginning of Psalm 46. But our God is bigger than the universe. There is nothing He can't handle or heal. There is nothing He can't do. I know that all cancer of the physical and spiritual kind has been defeated at the cross of Christ.

"The LORD himself goes before you and will be with you; he will never leave you nor forsake you. Do not be afraid; do not be discouraged." Deuteronomy 31:8

CHAPTER 8
Surgery and Recovery

I remember my first visit to Yale. My sisters Peggy and Wendy came with me. This was my last ditch effort to find someone who would actually do the surgery. While my sisters waited in the lobby, I met the surgeon for the first time. He introduced himself and said he'd been reading up on me and felt like he knew me. Compared to the last three visits, this was a very positive start to the appointment. After talking about his take on the medical reports he said something that I had been dying (pun intended) to hear after visiting three other hospitals. He said there were several different ways he could do a urinary diversion. It took me a couple minutes before I realized he was half way through the surgery and I hadn't even hired him yet. I didn't expect this kind of reception. This doctor was exactly what Jesus, the Great Physician ordered.

My sisters came in and were brought up to speed on what needed to be done. The bladder needed to come out, along with a full hysterectomy. The doctor and I agreed that creating the urinary diversion via the ilieal conduit would be best for me. It meant I would have an ostomy bag for the rest of my life. The doctor also offered a solution to my weight. He would have a plastic surgeon come in and take off excess weight around my abdomen. This would make his job easier and would cut down on a lot of complications and infections. After prompting from my sisters, "Rose, it's a free tummy tuck, say yes", I said yes.

You have to understand that my family comes from a long line of very humorous descendants. My grandmother was from Scotland, so she had that great Scottish humor which was passed down through my mom. My grandfather on Dad's side was from Texas, which is where we got the "Graff" crazy humor. So it wasn't too shocking to hear my sister Peggy ask the doctor "Can you get a family group rate on the tummy tuck? We have another one back at home." There was actual laughing in the room. The last place I thought I would hear it. I had come from doom and gloom to actual hope.

God can bring joy and laughter through any situation in our lives. He puts people there to implement that joy and laughter. I thank Him that Peggy and Wendy were there. I felt like skipping out of the office. I told my sisters that this was the best doctor's appointment I ever had. After working out the logistics, I was having the surgery less than three weeks later.

Just because God did not heal me supernaturally, didn't mean that he stopped being involved with my illness. It is truly undeniable that God orchestrated the events that led me to the right hospital and the right physician to do the job.

The day finally came for the surgery and it was a huge undertaking. My niece Cassie drove me to Yale early in the morning on Friday, October 14th, a day I will never forget. My sister in-law, Heidi, met us there for support. Then there were the onslaught of doctors, nurses and interns. They all came in one by one to ask me the same questions over and over again. Questions like, what is your name and do you know where you are and why you are here. It was both tiring and intimidating. After all, their job was to make sure they had the right patient and were going to remove the correct organ. I appreciated that.

My entrance into the operating room (OR) was quite different from the old days. Before, they would sedate you in your room and wheel you in on a gurney. Now, you just walk in. Here's your cap and slippers, follow me. As I left Cass and Heidi, I felt overcome with emotions. I gave them each a hug as if I wasn't going to see them again. As the anesthesiologist started to escort me to the OR, I heard Heidi saying, "God's got this, God's got this." I thought my faith was intact. But I guess we all have our moments. I was still kind of hoping for a miraculous healing from the hand of God as I walked down the long hallway that seemed to go on forever. As I said before, I am not afraid to die. But when I think about it, I feel sadness. Not for me, but for my loved ones.

> In our darkest fears, God will always be there waiting for us to come to him in complete submission.

The OR itself is very intimidating. There were a lot of instruments that I just couldn't bring myself to imagine what each one was going to be used for. As I sat on the OR table while the assistants and interns prepped for the surgery, I felt a familiar peace come over me. The kind of peace that reassured me that Someone greater and far more capable than the medical staff was in the room and in complete control.

It is truly amazing how God can work in your life. Sometimes it's easier to struggle with Him than to submit to His plan. That's because you think that you are still in control while that struggle goes on. But in reality, He is the one in control. And eventually His love wins you over. God stands ready to give us grace, peace, calmness and assurance that even though our world seems like it's turned upside down, His is still right side up. That is because He is still on His throne, in complete control.

With that peace from God, I finally submitted my circumstance to Him. And whenever you do that, all fear flees. In our darkest fears, God will always be there waiting for us to come to Him in complete submission. When the time came, I laid down on the table. When they put the mask on me to administer the anesthesia, I started to pray out loud, even though I knew no one in the room could hear me. I just wanted to hear myself to make sure I would remember what I said. So, with the peace that surpasses all understanding, I prayed to my heavenly Father. "Father, my life is in your hands. I trust you. Please be the great physician that you are and heal me in whatever way you choose." Then I passed out. I will never forget that moment. I know the spirit of the Lord was in that place. I know the same promise that Jesus made to His disciples was the same promise that he was making to me. It was the one He gave me when I was struggling with my kidney cancer.

"Peace I leave with you; my peace I give you. I do not give to you as the world gives. Do not let your hearts be troubled and do not be afraid." John 14:27

The recovery was even more amazing. The doctor said the surgery would be about 5-6 hours long; I could be intubated for up to three days in the ICU after the surgery and I could be in the hospital for up to 14 days, none of which happened. The surgery was between four and five hours. Evidently the doctors were ecstatic over how well the surgery went. They brought me straight from the OR to recover for about four hours. Then they took me to my room where my family was waiting for me. We talked, mostly laughed, and had a great time.

My sister Amy spent one night in the room with me after the surgery. That was fun. Many friends visited me from church including several visits from my Pastors. Peggy and her husband Gerry came by for a visit. One afternoon my brother Ken came to visit me. We had a wonderful time of fellowship and prayer before he left. Then came the day to go home which was day nine. I would have to say that my stay at Smilow was the best hospital experience I ever had. The staff was wonderful. They were always upbeat, understanding and very patient. God is truly good. Not once did He leave my side. I am forever grateful for His presence which is never ending.

Then there is my mom. After going through stage 3 lung cancer herself she came up from South Carolina and stayed with me for the two month recovery. That was a great sacrifice. But what mom wouldn't do that for her child.

It is clear to me and I hope it is clear to you that God's hand was in all of this from the beginning to the end.

Prayer Letter

Dear God;

Thank you for all the people you put in my path as I journey through my own cancer in life, from my family and friends, to co-workers as well as those in the medical field that you use to heal. Remind me that through them, your love for me is obvious. Most of all, thank you for the peace that transcends all human understanding.

With a grateful heart,

_____

Your name

I will praise You, O Lord, with all my heart;
before the "gods" I will sing your praise.
Psalm 138:1

CHAPTER 9

Providence and Praise

God's providence in my life becomes clearer with every battle that comes my way. Psalm 138 expresses the Lord's love for me and the praise that fills my heart for Him.

I will praise You, O Lord, with all my heart;
before the "gods" I will sing your praise.

I will bow down toward your holy temple
and will praise your name
for your love and your faithfulness,
for you have exalted above all things
your name and your word.

When I called, You answered me;
you made me bold and stouthearted.

May all the kings of the earth praise You, O Lord,
when they hear the words of your mouth.

May they sing of the ways of the Lord,
for the glory of the Lord is great.
Though the Lord is on high, He looks upon the lowly,
but the proud he knows from afar.

Though I walk in the midst of trouble,
you preserve my life; you stretch out your hand
against the anger of my foes,
with your right hand you save me.

The Lord will fulfill his purpose for me;
your love, O Lord, endures forever—
do not abandon the works of your hands.

"The fear of the Lord is the beginning of wisdom; all who follow His precepts have good understanding. To Him belongs eternal praise." Psalm 111:10

CHAPTER 10

Learning from My Walk With Cancer and Jesus

Cancer has a way of making you more sensitive to life. And I don't mean just the color of the sky or trees. But sensitive to the people you love. Jesus' command is clear in Luke 10:27.

"Love the Lord your God with all your heart and with all your soul and with all your strength and with all your mind; and, love your neighbor as yourself."

The order of things is to love God, then others as yourself. Most preachers focus on the first step which is to love God with all your heart, mind, soul and strength. I believe that we cannot love others or even

> The Lord is the one with the sovereign power over life and death.

ourselves until we have experienced God's love for us, which is unconditional through the cross of Christ. Once we have accepted His unconditional love the rest just follows. Then we can impart that same unconditional love to others, including a healthier love for ourselves.

I found myself extremely sensitive to the little things that people did for me during my cancer. Someone sent me an email saying they were praying for me and I started to cry. The first week at home was a little challenging. It was a couple of weeks before I could take a shower. So my sister Peggy washed my hair in the kitchen sink. It felt good just to have clean hair. It was a very simple thing, but it meant the world to me. Later, Peg emailed me and said it was a blessing to her to wash my hair. It reminded her of Jesus washing the disciple's feet at the last supper. Jesus calls us to the most ordinary and mundane tasks of life, the kind we would normally overlook because of their simplicity. But Jesus doesn't overlook such things. He commends the hearts of his servants. And my sister Peggy is definitely one of them.

My sister Wendy was wonderful as well. She made several trips to the grocery store for mom and me. She would come over and check on us periodically. I wasn't home long before we got hit with a freak October snow storm which put most of our state in the dark for several weeks, just what I needed after major surgery. Wendy and her husband Bob came to pick up mom and myself and let us camp in their living room for almost 2 weeks. Needless to say they had power. Yes, my family and friends were wonderful to me. I still feel God's love through their kind actions and words. It makes me think that I had been taking advantage of them before my episode with cancer.

By taking advantage I mean not appreciating them as much as I do now. God has healed me of this cancer. Now that I have a greater appreciation for my own life, I find myself seeking God's definition of what it really means to "love your neighbor as yourself". This starts with being sensitive to others needs as they were with mine. I also found that my love for my family and friends deepened tremendously, which I believe is a continuous gift from God.

There are so many other things I learned from both of my cancers. Actually, they are things I learned from Jesus during my time with cancer. He taught me a long list of where cancer (or other undesirable circumstances) can take you. It can take you down the road of bitterness, anger, sadness, fear, and an uncertain future. It can make you withdraw from family and friends. It can cause you to feel depressed, lonely, abandoned. And it can make you feel like your spirit and soul have been crushed. Ultimately, it can make you question God's love for you.

Some of these things I've experienced. Some of them I did not experience because of my knowledge of who God is. God has one answer to all of these negative feelings. It is simple.

"Come to me, all you who are weary and burdened, and I will give you rest. Take my yoke upon you and learn from me, for I am gentle and humble in heart, and you will find rest for your souls." Matthew 11:28-29

This is a loaded promise from Jesus. In the above scripture, Jesus' heart is revealed. First, He invites us into His presence. His heart breaks for us when we go through painful circumstances, just as His heart breaks over our sin. While we are still here on this earth, none of us are exempt from consequences of our sins, other people's sin or from the consequential impact of humanity's sin in the world, like disease and natural disasters. When human sin entered into the world through Adam and Eve, the whole earth suffered and continues to suffer until the day Jesus comes and makes all things new. But through the Holy Spirit, we can experience God's peace through the most horrifying and challenging circumstances we find ourselves in.

He then offers us rest, not just from the burden of our sins, but times of distress and trouble as well. Sometimes we find rest once we see our circumstance from a different perspective. And God's perspective is always different from ours.

He also offers help to carry our burdens by calling us to take His yoke upon us. When the weight of the load is too much for an animal to pull, he gets paired up with another of his kind by using a wooden yoke. This way, they both carry the weight together. When we are "yoked" together with Christ, we no longer need to carry the burden alone.

Remember, the one who died for us on the cross is now seated at the right hand of the Father in heaven. He is the one who intercedes on our behalf when it comes to our sin. He is also the only doorway to the altar of the God of the Universe. It is at this throne and this throne alone that we can find rest and peace. It is the power of the Holy Spirit that can give us strength to carry on through our circumstance. I have never depended on God as much in the past as I have during my bladder cancer.

This is the place where we also learn from God. I don't know how anyone can stand so close to God and not learn from Him, or walk away unchanged.

"Oh, the depth of the riches of the wisdom and knowledge of God! How unsearchable his judgments, and his paths beyond tracing out! Romans 11:33

When it comes down to it, my cancer and yours is bigger than both of us put together. I learned that cancer doesn't just wreak havoc in our bodies, but our minds, emotions and spirit as well. Who better than the God of the universe to call on to come to our rescue from the day to day burdens of the "cancers" of life.

"Therefore I tell you, do not worry about your life, what you will eat or drink; or about your body, what you will wear. Is not life more important than food, and the body more important than clothes? Look at the birds of the air; they do not sow or reap or store away in barns, and yet your heavenly Father feeds them. Are you not much more valuable than they? Who of you by worrying can add a single hour to his life?" Matthew 6:25-34.

Finally, I learned that God is the one that counts the number of hairs on our heads, not the cancer. No disease, plane crash, car accident or weapon will take our lives before the allotted time God set forth before we were even born. The Lord is the one with the sovereign power over life and death.

"The word of the Lord came to me, saying, 'Before I formed you in the womb I knew you, before you were born I set you apart;'"
Jeremiah 1:4-5

"The Lord brings death and makes alive; He brings down to the grave and raises up." 1 Samuel 2:6

If God wanted to call me home to heaven, no amount of medicine or science would have saved my physical body. But the Lord chose not to take me home. And if God chooses not to take you home to heaven today, then He will move heaven and earth to show you where you need to go and what you need to do to stay alive. That's what He did for me. Jesus alone gave me the strength and courage to fight on for my life. And he will give you the strength and courage to fight through the battle that you are currently in as well.

Prayer Letter

Dear God;

Forgive me for being so ignorant of your Word. Your ways are so much higher than mine. Help me to see my circumstance through your sovereign eyes from the beginning to the end. Please hold my hand as we go through this together and never let go of me.

Forever trusting you,

_____

Your name

"Praise be to the God and Father of our Lord Jesus Christ, the Father of compassion and the God of all comfort, who comforts us in all our troubles, so that we can comfort those in any trouble with the comfort we ourselves have received from God. For just as the sufferings of Christ flow over into our lives, so also through Christ our comfort overflows. If we are distressed, it is for your comfort and salvation; if we are comforted, it is for your comfort, which produces in you patient endurance of the same sufferings we suffer. And our hope for you is firm, because we know that just as you share in our sufferings, so also you share in our comfort."
2 Corinthians 1:3-7

CHAPTER 11

My Cancer as a Blessing

Since the surgery in October of 2011, I have been to the oncologist every three months for a CAT scan. At first there was a lymph node that was 1.1 cm that he was concerned about. Evidently it was swollen from the surgery because it eventually went down. The 17 lymph nodes the surgeon removed were all clean as well as the margins. Though the cancer started to spread into the fatty tissue of the cervical area, the surgeon was able to clean that area out when he did the hysterectomy.

The oncologist was extremely helpful with information regarding the return of the cancer. He said the first milestone is the first two years. I was stage 4 which means the percentage is high for the cancer to return. However, the longer I go without the cancer returning, the lower the percentage of reoccurrence. So far I have not needed any treatment other than the surgery, which to my understanding is unusual for someone with that type of cancer.

Once again, this confirms to me that God is in complete control. I am totally in His hands, as we all are. I told the doctor that I was not going to keep looking over my shoulder. I have a life to live and I am going to live it. He agreed. I also told him that Squamous Cell is in God's hands. All through this book I have said that I am not afraid to leave this world. Whatever my future holds, it is being held in the palm of the hand of the one who created the heavens and the earth.

I am grateful for my cancer. That's right. You don't have to go back and read it again. I said I am grateful for my cancer. I actually miss my time with cancer. Don't get me wrong, I don't miss the cancer itself. The greatest blessing through this whole ordeal is I have encountered God on a deeper level than before. I have experienced a relationship with Him that I might not have if I didn't have cancer. I have learned so much about His sovereignty over my life and His love for me. Cancer has allowed me to experience His love, grace, mercy and healing in a more profound way. And in that experience, He guided me through it all. I have found that only the light of God's presence can outshine the darkness of cancer.

He continues to show me the little blessings from my cancer which, are really big blessings. The symptoms of the bladder cancer would wake me up four or five times a night, feeling like I had to go to the bathroom, but I never could. I went for months without getting a good night sleep. Now that I have an ostomy bag, all I do is connect the bag to a larger one which allows me to sleep all night, which is a huge blessing. Another blessing is I am still able to swim which I love to do every chance I get. That may seem like a very insignificant thing, but God has a way of turning those things that we take for granted into huge blessings.

Jesus has walked me through my cancer. He has seen me through the entire journey and has made himself more real to me than ever before. So what now? I do not believe that this journey of living with cancer and Jesus was just for my benefit. God had a purpose.

"Praise be to the God and Father of our Lord Jesus Christ, the Father of compassion and the God of all comfort, who comforts us in all our troubles, so that we can comfort those in any trouble with the comfort we ourselves have received from God." 2 Corinthians 1:3-4

God allows things in our lives that we may never understand. But that does not mean He is not close to us. That does not mean He has withdrawn His grace or love from us either. His comfort is always there. This truth I believe; whatever we go through in life we are called to a higher purpose by God to share the hope that comes from our Lord and Savior Jesus Christ. Not just the peace that comes through trusting Him while we live our lives here on earth, but the hope of a future eternity with God that is promised throughout the Bible. Don't get me wrong. If God asked my opinion on the whole matter and said that people would be helped by it, I certainly would have said no to the bladder cancer. Who wouldn't? But that is just my selfish, human disposition. So for our own good, thank God He doesn't ask our opinion.

I am glad Jesus didn't say no to His cancer, which was our sin. He had a lot of opportunities to do so. If he chose to be disobedient to the Father, then we would have every reason to fear death. Paul, the author of the book of Philippians states it well of Jesus:

"Who, being in very nature God did not consider equality with God something to be grasped, but made himself nothing, taking the very nature of a servant, being made in human likeness. And being found in appearance as a man, he humbled himself and became obedient to death even death on a cross!" Philippians 2:6-8

In obedience, Jesus' love for the Father and love for us drove Him to the cross, the greatest and most unconditional love humanity can ever experience. There are two reasons I believe that God wanted me to write this book. First, that you know you are not alone in your cancer. There are millions of us out there going through the same thing, so be encouraged and don't be ashamed or afraid to talk about it or reach out for help. Second, I write this book so that you may know there is hope in life and death through the unconditional love of God that is in Christ.

My prayer is that you experience His forgiveness and the peace he offers through life's trials. Also, that you may know that there is nothing to fear in death. After seeing the hand of God through this whole ordeal, I believe this now more than ever. The God that held my hand down here through my cancer will be there to greet me into His kingdom when He calls me home. Place your faith in Jesus, and He will be there to greet you too.

I want to leave you with a verse from one of my favorite songs. It is packed with God's truth. May God bless you with good health and His Mighty Presence.

No guilt in life, no fear in death
This is the power of Christ in me

From life's first cry, to final breathe
Jesus commands my destiny

No power of hell or scheme of man
can ever pluck me from His hand

'Till he returns or calls me home
here in the love of Christ I stand

"In Christ Alone"
Words and Music by Keith Getty and Stuart Townend

Made in the USA
Lexington, KY
14 December 2019